Spongeware and Spatterware

Kevin McConnell

1469 Morstein Road, West Chester, Pennsylvania 19380

6½" barrel-form pitcher with vivid blue sponging on white earthenware. Circa 1910. *Value:* $90.00-$120.00+.

Title page photo:
Handleless tea cup with coarse pink and blue spattering. This is an excellent transitional example between spatterware and spongeware. 2½" high, 4" rim diameter. Circa 1830. *Value:* $70.00-$95.00.

Published by Schiffer Publishing, Ltd.
1469 Morstein Road
West Chester, Pennsylania 19380
Please write for a free catalog
This book may be purchased from the publisher.
Please include $2.00 postage.
Try your bookstore first.

Printed in the United States of America.
ISBN: 0-88740-253-4

Contents

This fancy serving bowl
with its scalloped rim and
heavy green sponging over
yellowware measures 3″
high and 6½″ in diameter.
Circa 1880. *Value:* $65.00-
$80.00.

Barrel shaped cookie jar with blue and rust sponging on the central band and the ear handles. 8″ high. Circa early 1900s. *Value:* $65.00-$85.00.

Acknowledgments

Writing an antique book is a bit like formulating a chemical equation. In this particular case, the "formula" consisted of three months of research and photography as well as 6000 miles of long and winding roads.

But without a doubt, the most important part of the book-writing formula are the collectors and dealers, whose accumulations form the very crux of this publication. Since I do not own a single object which appears in this book, I was wholly reliant upon the kindnesses of said collectors and dealers in my efforts to photograph the necessary pieces.

It has been my happy experience that collectors of antique ceramics are among the most helpful, knowledgeable, and trusting of people. Listed on the following page are the many fine folks that contributed to this endeavor, and it is to them that I dedicate this book.

Custard cups with light green and brown sponging. The example on the left is 1½" high and 4" diameter, while the one on the right is 2" high and 3¼" diameter. Circa 1910. *Value:* $15.00-$25.00 each.

Pennsylvania and New York State: Seymour and Violet Altman, Antiques at the Barn, Amy Bevevino, Sue Burke, Callender's Antiques, Mrs. Lena Eyrich, Hazel M. Fiedler, Jim and Eileen Goodling, Fran Johnson, Bill and Lewis Keister Antiques, John and Marilyn Kubalak, Katherine McAndrews, Mr. and Mrs. C. H. McConnell, Mizzentop Farm Antiques, Vance T. Nailor Antiques, Mrs. Evelyn Norberg Antiques, Nick and Joanne Nosel, Olde Brick Antiques, Dave and Vi Ristau, Pam Schmader, John R. and Lane Snedden, Craig Taylor, Linda Lee Vertacino, Betsie Yerkes, Zettle's Antiques.

Texas and Oklahoma: Azle Antique Mall, John Bennett, Burleson Antique Mall, Bob and Georgia Caraway, Robert Gordon, Mark and Lucy Greene, Bill and Maurine Livingston, Robert Wyman Newton, Mike Pennington, Marlene Stolte, Les and Sue Thompson, Aurelia Wikoff.

6" high cracker jar made by the Roseville Pottery Company during the early 1900s. Strong blue sponging over white earthenware. Note the unusual gold overglaze sponging. *Value:* $90.00-$115.00.

Introduction

The Joy of Spongeware and Spatterware

Antique and collectible ceramics of all kinds hold a very strong appeal for me, but if I had to play favorites, it would be spongeware and spatterware that won the prize. There's a lot to like about them— vivid colors, attractive shapes, and a history of manufacture and usage that is as long as it is fascinating.

Another reason that I like them so much is that they are truly forms of folk art, since they were all decorated by hand and no two pieces are quite the same.

Consequently, spongeware and spatterware have a visual impact that lends itself to an infinite variety of decorative possibilities. Whether a modern or a country setting, whether a single piece or a collection, sponge and spatter have a knack for looking great.

Blue spatterware creamer (3¾" high) and sugar bowl (3¼" high). *Value:* $120.00-$150.00 set.

These endearing qualities have perpetuated an interest in and appreciation for these wares that has spanned over 150 years and several generations. Today, they are more popular than ever, earning them a well-deserved place in the world of antiques and collectibles.

Which brings us to the why and the wherefore of this book. In the pages that follow, you will find a brief history of spongeware and spatterware as well as a few collecting tips. For the most part, I've tried to keep the text basic and minimal, as I feel that the photos speak quite clearly for themselves. Researching this book has provided a fine learning opportunity for me, and I sincerely hope that you enjoy the finished product as much as I did writing and photographing it.

Highly relief-molded pitcher with coarse blue spattering. The form strongly suggests that this item is of English origin. Circa 1830. *Value:* $300.00- $350.00.

A Word About Pricing

I must admit, with all due honesty, that trying to place legitimate values on the hundreds of objects that appear in this book was something of a difficult task.

In an effort to do so, I checked, double-checked, and variously cross-referenced spongeware and spatterware values via every current antiques and collectibles price guide known to humankind.

The intended goal, of course, was to come up with a realistic price range for each and every piece. I truly believe that, for the most part, the values presented herein are pretty close to the mark.

5" high, 7½" diameter spittoon with strong blue sponging and banding. While most collectors tend to shun spittoons, examples like this are avidly sought. Circa 1860. *Value:* $90.00-$120.00.

However, let me be quick to caution that these are *average* price ranges, and that there are many places in the country where spongeware and spatterware prices far exceed the average.

I found this to be particularly true of Eastern Pennsylvania, where blue and white spongeware was often twice as expensive as it tends to be in the Midwest and Southwest.

Obviously, it is impossible for me to compensate for such pricing extremes other than to make mention of them, and assume that folks in such areas are accustomed to buying and selling spongeware and spatterware for higher prices than I've reflected in this book. In closing, let me recommend that you build your spongeware and spatterware collection with objects that are pleasing to your eye and environment, rather than buying pieces simply because they are valuable.

Two gallon stoneware water cooler decorated with blue sponging. Height 9½", diameter 10". Circa 1900. *Value:* $135.00-$175.00+.

Spongeware and Spatterware Terminology

Spatterware: Originated and manufactured in the Staffordshire district of England from around 1780 to 1830, spatterware is the progenitor of spongeware pottery. Spatterware is identifiable by specific design themes or patterns which are accented by sophisticated, controlled spatterwork. Almost all spatterware is English, although rare American examples are known to exist.

Spongeware: It is the generally accepted theory that spongeware metamorphosed from spatterware as a result of the need to speed the decorating process. The outcome was a coarser, simpler style of decor which was quickly achieved by daubing colors onto the ware with either cut sponges, brushes, or pieces of cloth. Although the earliest examples of spongeware are English, this ware was quickly adopted by the fledgling American pottery industry and became a mainstay of factory production and household use until around 1930.

These three examples clearly illustrate the transition from spongeware (left) to rockinghamware (middle) to brownware (right).

Red Wing stoneware bowl with spongeband decoration. 4¼" high, 7¼" diameter at rim. Circa 1920. *Value:* $40.00-$55.00.

Red Wing: Located in Red Wing, Minnesota, the Red Wing Union Stoneware Company manufactured large quantities of utilitarian pottery during the early 20th century. Among their products was a distinctive type of spongeware which is characterized by rust and blue sponging on white. This sponging often appears in the form of a slender band of colors. Red Wing spongeware is sometimes signed on the base with an ink-stamp potter's mark.

East Liverpool, Ohio: During its heyday in the 1890s, this clay and coal rich region was the largest pottery producing center in the United States. East Liverpool came to be known as "Crockery City" due to their prodigious output, which included yellowware, rockinghamware, and much spongeware.

Rockinghamware: Not to be confused with spongeware, rockinghamware consists of a caramel-colored glaze over yellowware or earthenware: said glaze is typified by a heavy, runny, random appearance, differentiating it from spongeware with its daubed-on, more controlled colorations.

"Chicken Wire" Sponging: A specific type of decoration characterized by brownish-rust and green sponging which appears in the form of irregular, overlapping concentrics, usually on yellow or buff-colored wares.

Spatterware The Forerunner of Spongeware

In order to discuss spongeware pottery, it is necessary to first chronicle the history of spatterware. The most important thing to remember about spatterware, is that it is the predecessor of spongeware.

While many dealers and collectors tend to lump spatterware and spongeware into one broad category, they are nonetheless distinctly different ceramic types, as will be explained.

To begin with, realize that spatterware had its genesis in the Staffordshire district of England during the late 18th century. Made from creamware or common earthenware, it included such diverse dinner

9¼" diameter blue spatterware bowl with Peafowl pattern *Value:* $325.00-$350.00.

pieces as: plates, bowls, cups and saucers, vegetable dishes, pitchers, tea and coffee pots, sugar bowls, and even miniatures.

The peak period of spatterware production was from 1810 to 1840, with much of it being exported to America as well as to Australia, South America, and even West Africa.

The primary factors that separate spatterware from spongeware are the types and the complexity of the decorations that are found on them.

While some spatterware was simply embellished with daubs of color, the vast majority of it bears specific patterns or motifs, with these examples being known as design spatterware.

Handleless cup and saucer with the Rose pattern and brown/black spattering. The saucer is 5½" in diameter, the cup is 2¾" high. *Value:* $150.00-$200.00.

Design spatterware is recognizable by the appearance of a hand-painted or transfer-printed theme in the center or on the sides of the ware, with the borders and the backgrounds being heavily accented by colorful spatterwork.

Some of the better known spatterware motifs are, Peafowl, Fort, Schoolhouse, Tulip, Thistle, and Acorn, with lesser known ones being, Cannon, Deer, Sailboat, Windmill, and Beehive.

Color is the chief value factor for spatterware: yellow and black are rare, while green, brown, and purple rate as the next rarest, and red and blue are by far the most common.

14

The spatterware process is thought to have been accomplished through the use of a fine brush, with the end result being as meticulous and sophisticated as it was time-consuming. In most cases, the desired spatterware effect involved hundreds of brush touches per square inch—all of which was done by hand.

Experts generally agree that by the 1830s, the laborious spatterware technique was no longer cost-effective or practical, thus giving way to a coarser, faster, less expensive manner of decorating. And so, spongeware came into being.

Much of the confusion of trying to differentiate spatterware from spongeware, comes from this initial period of transition, which produced items with overlapping attributes.

But for the most part, spatterware is quite different from spongeware for the following reasons.

—Most spatterware is older than spongeware and bears highly sophisticated design work.

—There is usually the presence of a recognizable pattern or decoration on most spatterware.

—Unlike spongeware, there is an absence of large open areas or white space on spatterware.

Remembering distinctions such as these is an important key to understanding the history of ceramics. Of course, since spatterware is so closely related to spongeware, it certainly makes for a logical and beautiful compliment to any spongeware assemblage.

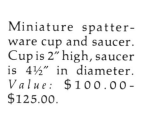

Miniature spatterware cup and saucer. Cup is 2″ high, saucer is 4½″ in diameter. *Value:* $100.00-$125.00.

8¾″ high tankard with highly controlled and detailed blue sponging. Circa 1850. *Value:* $175.00-$225.00+.

Evaluating and Pricing Spongeware

Because of its vivid colors and strong country charm, spongeware is currently one of the most popular items in the realm of antique collecting. Consequently, a conscious effort has been made to represent the true market values of the myriad examples pictured within this book.

Bearing the above in mind, it is imperative that the would-be spongeware collector understand that there are three primary value factors as regards spongeware pottery.

First and foremost is the matter of color. Without a doubt, the most popular and expensive of all sponge-

Relief-molded vegetable dish with heavy blue sponging over white earthenware. 9" long, 6½" wide, 1¾" deep. Circa 1840. *Value:* $145.00-$180.00.

Almost identical in form, these two pitchers clearly illustrate what an important value factor the strength of the sponging can be. Exhibiting very light coloration, the pitcher on the left is worth around $50.00, while the more vivid example on the right is valued at twice as much.

ware pottery is blue on white. Examples bearing this color combination are generally worth two to three times as much as pieces found in other colors, such as green on yellowware or brown on white.

Also highly valued are spongeware items displaying three colors, these for example being, green and brown on white, or red and blue on white.

With the above exceptions, most other two-color spongeware can still be purchased for a moderate sum. New collectors are advised to invest in these currently inexpensive examples now, as spongeware's popularity will eventually inflate the prices of even common pieces. In addition to color, condition is a major consideration in terms of a spongeware purchase. Ideally, one would like for all of the items in their collection to be in perfect, mint condition, but this is simply not possible. It is impossible, because most collectible spongeware is well over fifty years old, and was intended for everyday utilitarian use.

Because of this, many of the surviving pieces bear the scars of use and abuse—a chip, a crack, or even a missing lid. As such, purchasing damaged examples

This 7⅞" high blue and white spongeware vase is highly unusual because of its form, the fact that it's hand-thrown, and due to the underlying base clay which is redware. Circa 1860. *Value:* $250.00-$300.00.

becomes an eventual necessity of spongeware collecting.

Even so, one must exercise good sense and judgement by passing up common spongeware items that are damaged, as they're certain to turn up again in better condition.

Conversely, you will want to go ahead and buy those rare or unusual pieces, damaged though they may be, as you may never again have another opportunity to do so.

Please realize, however, that damaged pieces of spongeware (even rare ones), should be priced accordingly. That is to say that cracked examples should be priced at around 60% of retail, while items with minor chips or missing lids should reflect a value of 75%—80% of the price that would normally be asked for a perfect piece.

Finally, there is the matter of rarity of form. Regardless of what you collect, some variations are rarer than others, and spongeware is no exception. In general, custard cups, bowls, and pitchers are quite common, while odd items such as inkwells, water coolers, and vases remain elusive.

See the spongeware rarity chart elsewhere in this book for more specific information regarding scarcity. On the whole, always try to purchase items of rarity and quality whenever possible. Not only will those unusual examples form the backbone of your spongeware collection, but they'll continue to accrue value at a much greater rate than the more common pieces.

Massive 12" high pitcher with bulbous body and vivid blue vertical sponging. Circa 1860. *Value:* $275.00-$325.00+.

Spongeware Reproductions

Let The Buyer Beware

As is typically the case with any popular antique or collectible, spongeware reproductions exist in prodigious quantities. These are generally limited to simple forms such as pitchers, bowls, and crocks, decorated with strong, basic color combinations like dark blue on white and dark brown on buff.

Most of this modern spongeware is the output of the R.R.P. Company or Robinson Ransbottom Pottery Company of Roseville, Ohio. Examples usually bear an ink-stamp potter's mark on the base and are otherwise recognizable as being new by the absence of any wear whatsoever.

As good as it may look, this butter crock is, in fact, a contemporary reproduction.

A genuine circa 1840 butter crock with crude blue ring sponging and stenciling. 4¾" high, 7¼" in diameter. *Value:* $150.00-$185.00.

They are high quality reproductions, but spongeware enthusiasts nevertheless need to be aware of this information so that they don't end up paying a big price for a new piece.

This happens more often than you might imagine, the most typical scenario being an antique dealer who does not specialize in ceramics, and innocently sells an equally uninformed customer a new piece of spongeware as something old and valuable.

Far less innocent and considerably more unscrupulous are the con men and women who take these modern examples of spongeware and forge the appearance of age by sandpapering the base and the surface which are then discolored through the application of ink or soot. These are then passed off on the innocent and the unsuspecting as true antiques.

Opposite page:
This 9" high pitcher made by the Robinson Ransbottom Pottery Company of Roseville, Ohio is a typical example of contemporary reproduction spongeware. Note the potter's marked base as well as the lack of wear.

People who have been collecting spongeware for a while are not going to be duped by these bogus items, but novice collectors may well be. For those new to spongeware collecting, the wisest thing to do is to buy from a reputable dealer who specializes in primitive ceramics. The items you buy may cost a bit more, but you'll be assured of what you're getting.

Bulbous earthenware batter pitcher with bold blue brush sponging, 6½" high. *Value:* $125.00-$150.00+.

Spongeware Rarity Chart

The following generalized chart lists most of the major spongeware forms and groups them according to relative rarity. Keep in mind that even the most common forms can be rare and valuable if they bear particularly vivid or unusual sponge decoration.

Group One/Common
Bowls, casserole dishes, chamber pots, cookie jars, creamers, custard cups, mugs, pitchers, and spittoons.

Group Two/Relatively Rare
Banks, bean pots, crocks, cups and saucers, jardinieres, jugs, match holders, mustard pots, plates, platters, salt boxes, and soap dishes.

4½" high, 7" long figural cow creamer with bold brown sponging. This is a very rare, delicate, and sought after example of spongeware. *Value:* $750.00-$900.00+.

Group Three/Rare

Coffee pots, compotes, figurines, inkwells, most miniatures, pitcher and bowl sets, umbrella stands, vases, water coolers, and items with unusual or exceptional sponging.

Two views of a 5½″ high, 9″ diameter covered baking dish. This is a rare and unusual spongeware item with many exceptional features, such as, a petal-form knob, blue-glazed interior, wire bail handle, strong blue exterior sponging, and the original matching lid. Notice also that the exterior of this piece is unglazed. Circa 1900. *Value: $225.00-$275.00.*

A Century of Spongeware
1830-1930

In so many ways, the word spongeware is a somewhat misleading term. Unlike most other pottery types, spongeware is named for its decoration rather than for the type of clay it is made from.

Adding to the confusion surrounding spongeware is the fact that it is truly a transitional ceramic—it is a direct descendant of spatterware: it originated and was made in England before eventually becoming a favorite ware of rural America: and it was formed from a wide range of clay types through an even wider range of manufacturing methods.

The earliest examples of spongeware are of English origin, these dating from circa 1815—1830. English pieces are generally recognizable as such because of

3½" deep, 9¼" diameter redware bowl with white slip and brown manganese sponging. *Value:* $90.00-$120.00.

A classic example of early American redware decorated with black manganese sponging. This mold measures 4" high and 10" in diameter. Circa 1830. *Value:* $65.00-$85.00.

the quality of the sponging which is very controlled and sophisticated. All in all, they are rather reminiscent of spatterware, but lack the typical design motif and are decorated in a more open style, leaving more white space.

The great majority of the spongeware that you're likely to see was made in America, and it is comparatively cruder in form and decor than the English examples. Because of its inherent appeal, spongeware was quickly adopted by American potters, who began manufacturing it as early as 1830.

Much of the earliest American spongeware was fashioned from redware clay, which was variously splotched and daubed with brownish-black manganese oxides. The passing of the redware era, followed by the discovery of yellowware and stoneware clays in the United States helped to realize the full range of potential for spongeware.

An American favorite, spongeware enjoyed a full century of production, displaying such vivid color combinations as, blue on white, brown on yellowware, green on white or yellow, and even tri-color examples.

While the name spongeware indicates that all of this ware was decorated with a sponge, the truth is that a variety of tools and techniques were employed. These included not only coarse sponges, but also many different types of brushes as well as pieces of cloth —all of which were used to daub the color onto the body of the item.

Some of the boldest and most sought after spongeware is that which was decorated in a crude concentric ring pattern, most of which dates from around 1840-1860. But it is the exception rather than the rule, as most spongeware was splotched and daubed with no particular pattern in mind.

Because there are few discernable patterns and because it is so rarely potter's marked, spongeware can be difficult to date other than in the approximate terms detailed below.

—Most sponged examples of redware date from around 1830 or earlier.

—Heavy-bodied blue and white pieces that were formed in crude, two-piece molds from stoneware or earthenware were made from around 1840-1860.

4½" high squat mug with applied handle and dark blue sponging. Circa 1850. *Value:* $125.00-$150.00.

5¾" high bean pot. This type of multi-colored sponging which appears in the form of crude, overlapping concentrics is known as "chicken wire" and it generally dates from the late 19th/early 20th century. *Value:* $150.00-$185.00.

—Much of the sponge-decorated yellowware is from the 1850-1880 period.

—Spongeware with traces of gilding are from the turn-of-the-century.

—Spongeware which is potter marked "Red Wing" is the product of the Red Wing Union Stoneware Company of Minnesota and dates from the early 20th century.

For the most part, historical records indicate that the bulk of the spongeware that we collect today was made by long-vanished potteries which operated in the states of Ohio, New Jersey, and Maryland—all of which are known for their fine clays.

Perhaps the most famous of these was the Roseville Pottery of Zanesville, Ohio. During the early 1900s, they manufactured large quantities of spongeware, which is not potter's marked, but is still attributable to them through the use of old production catalogs.

Roseville spongeware included such lines as Cornelian and Colonial, which besides being sponge-

5" high, 8½" diameter mixing bowl. Green sponging on yellow-ware clay, traces of gilding around rim. Circa 1900. *Value:* $75.00-$95.00.

8¼" high baluster-form vase with blue glaze and dark blue and rust sponging. Circa 1910. *Value:* $90.00-$135.00.

Piggy banks, the example in the background measures 3" high, 5¾" long and is unmarked Roseville Pottery, while the one in the foreground is 2" high, 4¼" long and is probably of Austrian origin. Both are circa 1900. *Value:* $55.00-$80.00 each.

decorated and gilded, featured relief-molded organic designs like wheat, flowers, leaves, and ears of corn. These lovely patterns highlighted various utilitarian forms, including: pitchers, toilet sets, and jardinieres.

Roseville likewise made sponge-decorated novelties, among them a monkey bottle, and a variety of banks in the forms of a beehive, a dog's head, a cat's head, a buffalo, an eagle's head, a lion's head, and the ubiquitous piggy.

Because of spongeware's longevity, the methods by which it was manufactured run the range from hand-molding and firing by the early American country potter to factory mass-production of the post-Industrial Revolution.

In any case, spongeware remained the everyday utilitarian ceramic of the average American family throughout most of the 19th century and on into the early 20th.

Spongeware's perennial appeal continues to the present day, as new generations of collectors seek it out. Warm, colorful, charming —just a few of the many reasons why it has been so very popular for so very long.

Enjoy.

Spatterware

8¼″ diameter bowl with dark purple spattering and hand-painted Tulip pattern center. *Value:* $200.00- $250.00.

3½" high, 7" diameter pink spatterware waste bowl. *Value:* $110.00-$135.00.

3½″ high creamer exhibiting extremely fine spatter and sponge decor. *Value:* $50.00-$70.00.

Pink spatterware cup and saucer decorated with hand-painted Peafowl pattern. Cup is 2½" high, saucer is 6" in diameter. *Value:* $275.00-$325.00.

Description: Handleless tea cup and matching saucer embellished with pink spatterware and blue flower. Value: $75.00-$100.00

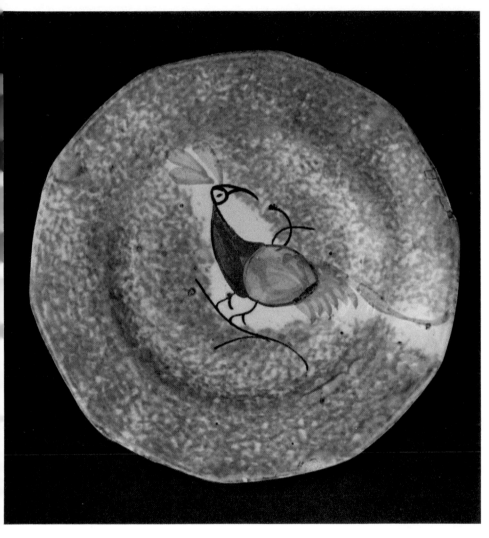

4″ diameter cup plate with blue spattering and hand-painted
Peafowl decor. *Value:* $100.00-$125.00.

10¼″ diameter spatterware plate with paneled edge and peafowl transfer in the center. Circa 1825. *Value:* $250.00-$300.00.

8¾″ diameter spatterware plate, decorated with a bull's-eye effect. *Value:* $125.00-$150.00.

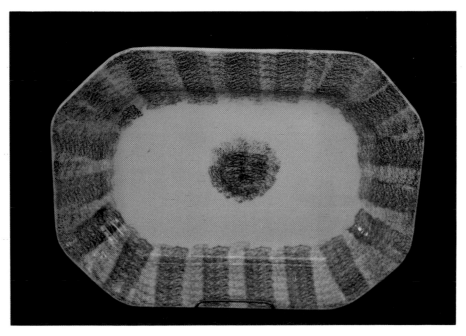

10½″ long, 8½″ wide octagonal platter with strong, distinctive rainbow spattering. *Value:* $300.00- $350.00.

5″ high pink and green spatterware sugar bowl.
Value: $140.00-$175.00 (with lid).

5″ high spatterware sugar bowl hand-decorated with the Fort pattern. *Value:* $250.00-$300.00.

5½" high blue spatterware sugar bowl complete with original lid.
Value: $175.00-$225.00.

42

Fancy, relief-molded, blue spatterware teapot. 7¼" high, 9½" long. *Value:* $120.00-$145.00+.

Blue and White Spongeware

Blue and white spongeware flower pot with attached saucer base. 5″ high, 5¼″ rim diameter. A rarity in spongeware. Circa 1850. *Value:* $200.00-$250.00.

Miniature blue and white spongeware cup and saucer. Cup is 1½" high, saucer is 3" in diameter. Circa 1850. *Value:* $150.00-$200.00.

Blue and white spongeware piggy bank, measuring 5" long and 3" high. Circa 1900. *Value:* $130.00-$150.00.

This beautifully blue-sponged bean pot complete with lid measures 6¼" high and 8" diameter. Circa 1850. *Value:* $300.00-$375.00.

Exceptionally large mixing bowl, 6" high and 12" diameter.
Embossed exterior with blue ring sponging. Circa 1860. *Value:*
$125.00-$150.00+.

Spongeware bowl with finely speckled coloration. 5" high, 9" rim
diameter. Circa 1910. *Value:* $40.00-$60.00.

1¾" high, 9" diameter soup bowl with heavy, dark blue overall sponging. Circa 1840. *Value:* $95.00-$135.00.

3" high, 9" diameter bowl with cut sponge highlighting. Circa 1850. *Value:* $120.00-$140.00.

4″ high, 6½″ diameter mixing bowl with blue sponging. Circa 1910. *Value:* $50.00-$65.00.

An enormous mixing bowl, measuring 7″ high and 15½″ in diameter. Blue sponging on white earthenware. *Value:* $125.00-$150.00.

Lidded casserole dish with heavy blue sponging. 4½" high, 9¾" in diameter. Circa 1930. *Value:* $85.00-$115.00.

Blue and white spongeware chamber pot with applied handle, 4½" high, 8" in diameter. Circa 1850. *Value:* $125.00-$150.00.

Three gallon crock with fine blue sponging over white stoneware. 11½" high, 10½" diameter. Circa 1900. *Value:* $160.00-$190.00

Miniature spongeware cup plate (4″ diameter) and handleless tea cup (2″ high). Circa 1840. *Value:* $90.00-$120.00 each.

5″ high honey jar with matching lid and dark blue sponging. This item originally had a wire handle which fit into the shoulder protrusions. *Value:* $95.00-$135.00+.

Blue and white spongeware planter. 3" high, 7" long. Circa 1930.
Value: $40.00-$60.00.

Bulbous jardiniere with blue sponging and banding. 6" high.
Circa 1860. *Value:* $300.00-$350.00.

Heavily sponged and gilded jardiniere measuring 9½" high and
10¼" rim diameter. Circa 1900. *Value:* $140.00-$175.00.

11″ high jug exhibiting dark blue sponging on a cream-colored ground. Circa 1910. *Value:* $200.00-$250.00+.

Hand-potted 6½″ high mug with flared rim and applied handle.
Blue sponging below the rim as well as on the handle. Circa 1890.
Value: $65.00-$80.00.

Made in a crude two-piece mold, this 9" high tankard exhibits beautiful dark blue sponging over white stoneware. Circa 1850. *Value:* $200.00-$250.00.

9″ high tankard with blue concentric ring sponging on white stoneware. Circa 1850. *Value:* $200.00-$250.00+.

9" high pitcher with relief-molded rose and vivid blue-on-white ring sponging. Circa 1850. *Value:* $250.00-$300.00+.

7" high pitcher with distinctive blue sponging. Circa 1860. *Value:* $150.00-$175.00.

7½" high pitcher exhibiting strong vertical brush sponging over white earthenware. *Value:* $125.00-$150.00+.

This fabulous example of spongeware features fine blue daubing on the top, bottom and handle of the pitcher with the embossed floral motif strongly emphasized in cobalt blue. 9" high. Circa 1850. *Value:* $250.00-$300.00+.

6½" high pitcher with blue daubing over white stoneware. Notice that the relief-molded "windowpane" design is actually a mold modification of the swastika or Indian peace symbol. Circa 1900. *Value:* $150.00-$185.00.

11¼″ high wash pitcher with blue sponging and banding. This piece would have originally had a matching bowl or basin. Circa 1850. *Value:* $150.00-$200.00+.

7" high pitcher with central blue banding and controlled rim and base sponging. Circa 1850. *Value:* $150.00-$200.00.

Octagonal stoneware pitcher with cut sponge decoration. 7½" high. *Circa* 1860. *Value:* $140.00-$180.00+.

6" high relief-molded syrup pitcher with blue daubing. Circa 1880. *Value:* $65.00-$90.00.

7" diameter blue and white spongeware plate. Circa 1860. *Value:* $60.00-$75.00.

8½" diameter dinner plate with scalloped, relief-molded edge and heavy blue sponging. Circa 1880. *Value:* $80.00-$95.00.

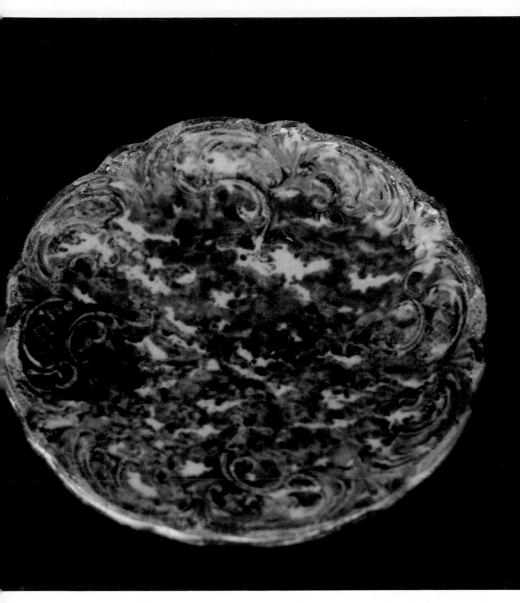

6" diameter plate, heavily relief-molded, sponged, and gilded. Circa 1890. *Value:* $70.00-$90.00.

11¼" long, 8" wide platter with scalloped, angled edges and heavy, dark blue sponging on white earthenware. Circa 1830. *Value:* $130.00-$165.00.

13" long, 9" wide oval platter with heavy overall blue sponging. Circa 1840. *Value:* $130.00-$150.00.

Blue and white spongeware soap dish measuring 5½" long and 3½" wide. Circa 1870. *Value:* $90.00-$120.00.

This unusual blue and white spongeware spittoon is shown with its original brass lid. 3½" high, 10¼" in diameter. *Value:* $175.00-$225.00.

Spittoon with relief-molded basket-weave exterior and blue ring sponging. Circa 1860. *Value:* $115.00-$140.00.

1¾" high toothpick or wooden match holder with thick bluish-pink sponging. Circa 1880. *Value:* $50.00-$75.00.

6" square blue and white spongeware trivet/tile. A rarity. Circa 1900. *Value:* $150.00-$200.00.

4¼″ high vase with bulbous body and strong blue sponging on white earthenware. Circa 1870. *Value:* $70.00-$90.00+.

Sponged Yellowware

Relief-molded bowl, 2" high, 5" diameter. Made from yellowware clay, it has a fluted base and a wide, paneled collar highlighted with green sponging. Circa 1900. *Value:* $20.00-$25.00.

Large mixing bowl with heavy brown sponging. The exterior exhibits relief-molded scrollwork. 5½" high, 10½" diameter. Circa 1870. *Value:* $85.00-$110.00.

This 2½" high, 9½" diameter spongeware bowl with its flat bottom and sloping sides functioned as a milk cooling basin. Circa 1870. *Value:* $60.00-$80.00.

Known as a "gypsy kettle", this item has an attached bail handle and is made from yellowware clay decorated with green sponging. 3¾" high, 6" greatest diameter. Late 19th century. *Value:* $65.00-$80.00.

This grouping consists of a small 2" high, 4¼" diameter bowl, and two 2" high custard cups. All are decorated with green and brown sponging. Circa 1900. *Value:* $25.00-$35.00 each.

Large serving bowl, 4¾" high, 10¼" diameter. Tan rim, bowl exterior decorated with "chicken wire" sponging. Circa 1900. *Value:*$70.00-$90.00

This serving bowl is desirable because of its odd ribbed and scalloped form as well as the alternating brown and green sponging. Circa 1880. *Value:* $90.00-$110.00.

Mixing bowl with brown sponging over yellowware. 10½"
diameter, 4½" high. Circa 1870. *Value:* $60.00-$80.00.

This odd example of spongeware exhibits brown coloration
which appears to have been brushed rather than daubed on. This
bowl is 2½" high and 6" in diameter. Circa 1880. *Value:* $30.00-
$45.00.

Small yellowware dish or custard cup with green sponging. 1¾" high, 3½" diameter. Circa 1890. *Value:* $15.00-$20.00.

Lidded butter crock with embossed florals on the lid, and peacock motif on the exterior. Brown sponging over cream-colored earthenware, 4¼" high and 6" diameter. Circa 1900. *Value:* $95.00-$125.00+.

Chamber pot with embossed grapes, leaves, and vines patterning the exterior. Both the interior and the exterior display heavy green sponging on yellowware. 6½" high, 11" greatest diameter. Circa 1910. *Value:* $75.00-$95.00.

5¼" high yellowware chamber pot with dark green sponging. Circa 1900. *Value:* $70.00-$85.00.

Relief-molded yellowware flower pot with vivid green copper oxide daubing. 6½" high, 6½" rim diameter. Circa 1910. *Value:* $110.00-$130.00

Fluted, leaf-form mold with speckled brown daubing on yellowware. 2½" high, 10¼" long. Circa 1870. *Value:* $95.00-$125.00.

9½″ jardiniere with ribbed exterior and strong green and brown sponging over yellowware. Circa 1900. *Value:* $120.00-$150.00.

Relief-molded yellowware mug with applied handle and strong brown sponging. 4¾" high. Circa 1870. *Value:* $50.00-$70.00.

3½" high shaving mug with green sponging over yellowware. Note the heavy gilding around the rim. Circa 1900. *Value:* $70.00-$90.00.

7¼". high pitcher exhibiting strong brown sponging on yellow-ware clay. Circa 1870. *Value:* $70.00-$90.00.

6½″ high milk pitcher with relief-molded rib exterior highlighted with green and brown sponging. Circa 1900. *Value:* $70.00-$85.00.

7" high pitcher with fancy, scalloped rim and bold tri-color sponging. Circa 1890. *Value:* $80.00-$95.00.

This 7″ high pitcher features embossed designs below the rim as well as brown sponging over yellowware clay. Circa 1870. *Value: $60.00-$70.00*

Squat 3¼″ high batter pitcher with applied handle and thick brown sponging over cream-colored earthenware. Circa 1870. *Value:* $40.00-$55.00.

9¼" high tankard with relief-molded latticework and barrel
hoops. Strong brown and green "chicken wire" sponging over
yellowware clay. Circa late 19th/early 20th century. *Value:*
$140.00-$160.00+

7¼″ high pitcher with strong brown sponging over yellowware clay. Circa 1870-1880. *Value:* $55.00-$70.00.

6" high pitcher and 9" diameter bowl, both with green sponging on yellowware clay. Vestiges of gilding apparent at rims of both pieces. Circa 1900. *Value:* $130.00-$175.00 for the set.

2¾" high bulbous creamer with applied handle and fine brown sponging. Circa 1870. *Value:* $50.00-$65.00+.

This wall-hanging salt box is 6" high, 5½" in diameter, and would have originally had a hinged walnut lid. A hard-to-find piece, which is particularly desirable for its tri-color sponging. Circa 1870. *Value:* $175.00-$195.00.

Yellowware spittoon with dark brown sponging. Measuring 5¼" high and 7¼" diameter at top, this particular item was made in a two-piece mold. Circa 1870. *Value:* $55.00-$70.00.

5¼" high sugar bowl with erratic brown sponging on yellowware. Circa 1870. *Value:* $125.00-$150.00.

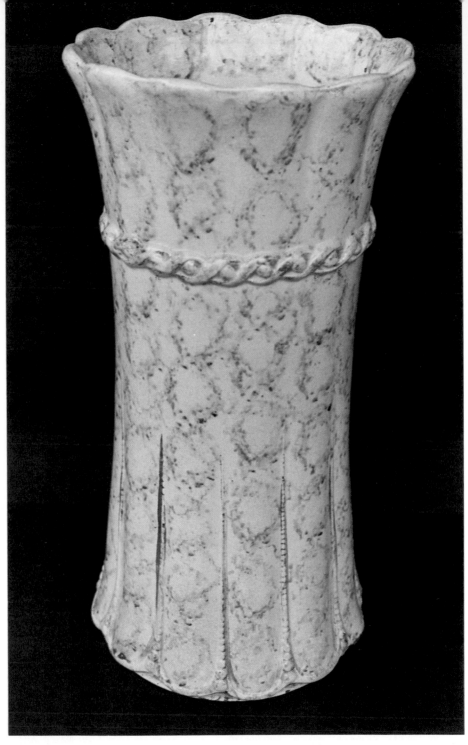

A massive relief-molded spongeware umbrella stand, which is
21″ high and 10″ in diameter. Circa 1900. *Value:* $450.00-
$500.00.

Bulbous yellowware vase covered with brown and green daubing. 4½" high. Circa 1900. *Value:* $70.00-$90.00.

4¾" high tumbler with dark brown sponging on yellowware. Probably part of a water set which once consisted of six such glasses as well as a pitcher. Circa 1870. *Value:* $40.00-$55.00.

8½" high bottle-
form vase with
green sponging
on yellowware.
Circa 1870.
Value: $125.00-
$165.00.

Brown and Green Spongeware

Soup bowl with embossed patterning on rim, and fine, brown sponging overall. 8" diameter, 2½" deep. Circa 1890-1910. *Value:* $30.00-$45.00.

Mixing bowl, 4½" high and 8¼" diameter. Green sponging on white earthenware. Circa 1900. *Value* $60.00-$75.00.

This 4½" high, 8" diameter mixing bowl displays the highly unusual combination of red banding and green sponging. Circa 1890. *value:* $80.00-$95.00.

3" high, 8¼" diameter basin with unusually fine brown sponging over white earthenware. Circa 1870. *Value:* $80.00-$95.00.

Matching set of three mixing bowls, shown both nested and as a grouping. These bowls have diameters of 7", 8" and 9½", and are 3½", 4" and 4½" high. All three bowls have banded exteriors and heavy brown and green daubing both inside and out. Circa early 1900s. *Value:* $95.00-$130.00 for the set.

3½" high, 9" diameter bowl with brown and green sponging and paneled exterior. Circa 1915. *Value:* $35.00-$45.00

Small dish or custard cup with brown and green sponging. 2" high, 4" in diameter. Circa 1910. *Value:* $20.00-$25.00.

Waste or slop jar with green sponging on yellowware. 4½" high, 6" rim diameter. Circa 1900. *Value:* $60.00-$85.00.

Measuring 2½" high and 3" in diameter, these brown-sponged custard cups are among the most commonly found examples of spongeware. Circa 1900. *Value:* $15.00-$20.00 each.

These small spongeware bowls are extremely common and inexpensive. 2" high, 5" in diameter. Circa 1900. *Value:* $18.00-$25.00 each.

2¼" deep, 9½" wide soup bowl with brown sponging on cream-colored earthenware. Circa 1900. *Value:* $35.00-$50.00.

Brown-sponged baking dish with bail handle and unglazed exterior. 4" high, 8½" in diameter. Circa 1890. *Value:* $110.00-$135.00.

Large mixing bowl with mottled green sponging on cream-colored earthenware. 5" high, 10½" in diameter. Circa 1900. *Value:* $55.00-$70.00.

Lidded casserole dish with relief-molded fluting. 5" high, 7½" diameter, brown and green sponging on cream-colored earthenware. Circa 1910. *Value:* $55.00- $70.00.

This handled casserole lid is collectible in and of itself, since it functioned separately as a serving dish/bowl when inverted. 7¾" diameter. Circa early 1900s. *Value:* $20.00-$25.00.

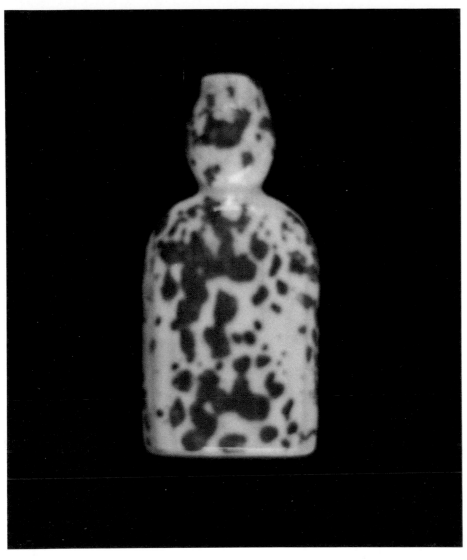

3¾″ high pocket flask with brown daubing. Circa 1910. *Value:* $55.00-$70.00.

Pitcher with pronounced spout and heavy brown and green
sponging over buff earthenware. 7¼" high. Circa 1900. *Value:*
$70.00-$90.00

4" high creamer and 3" high custard cup, both with dark green sponging on cream-colored earthenware. Circa 1900. *Value:* Creamer: $45.00-$60.00. Custard cup: $25.00-$35.00

4½" high creamer with pronounced spout, and 2" high custard cup: both with brown and green sponging. Circa early 1900s. *Value:* Creamer: $25.00-$35.00. Custard cup, $18.00-$25.00.

7" high barrel-form pitcher with brown and green sponging. This particular form was a great favorite among potters during the late 19th/early 20th century, and consequently can be found in an amazing array of glazes and colors. Circa 1915. *Value:* $70.00-$80.00.

4½″ high creamer with relief-molded exterior, brown and green sponging, and transfer-printed advertising. Originally given away as gifts or premiums, advertising spongeware has become a popular area of collecting. Circa 1920. *Value:* $45.00-$60.00.

Spongeware advertising creamer, 4½″ high. Note the oddity of the advertising, which has a strong bearing on the value of such items. Circa 1920. *Value:* $55.00-$70.00.

9″ diameter dinner plate with finely sponged edge. Circa 1910. *Value:* $65.00-$85.00.

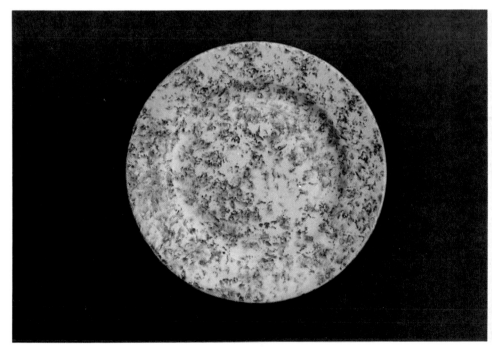

6″ diameter plate with tight brown sponging over cream-colored earthenware. Circa 1900. *Value:* $35.00-$50.00.

4½″ high octagonal sugar bowl with applied ears and dark brown sponging. Circa 1860. *Value:* $140.00-$175.00 (with lid).

Teapot with brown and green daubing over cream-colored earthenware. 5½" high, 9" long. Circa early 1900s. *Value:* $75.00-$95.00.

6" high teapot with fluted exterior and brown and green sponging. Circa 1910. *Value:* $90.00-$110.00 (with lid).

Roseville and Red Wing Spongeware

4" high relief-molded dog's head bank made by the Roseville Pottery Company. Circa 1900. *Value:* $125.00 -$150.00.

6" high, 10¾" diameter bowl with rust and blue sponging. Probably Red Wing. Circa 1910. *Value:* $85.00-$95.00.

This 5½″ high, 9½″ diameter Red Wing spongeware bowl is particularly desirable because of the advertising which appears on the interior. Items like this were usually given away as premiums. *Value:* $90.00-$110.00.

Red Wing baking dish with fluted exterior and blue and rust sponging. 4¼" high, 7" diameter. Also pictured is the potter's-marked base. Circa 1930. *Value*: $50.00-$60.00.

Red Wing spongeband casserole dish, 3¼" high and 6½" diameter. Base exhibits ink-stamp potter's mark. *Value:* $50.00-$65.00.

5" high, 7¾" diameter crock heavily decorated with blue and rust sponging. Circa 1890. *Value:* $90.00-$115.00.

Storage crock with original lid and tri-color sponging. 7½" high and 7¾" diameter. Circa 1880. *Value:* $150.00-$175.00+.

This 9" high spongeware jardiniere is a beautiful example of the Roseville Pottery's "Cornelian" line, and it dates from the early 1900s. *Value:* $100.00- $120.00.

4½" high mug, hand-thrown with applied handle and dark blue and rust sponging. Circa 1880. *Value:* $100.00-$125.00.

5" high Roseville "Cornelian" pitcher with embossed ear of corn, blue and rust sponging, and gilded highlights. Circa 1910. *Value:* $65.00-$80.00.

5″ high bulbous pitcher with tricolor blue, pink, and brown sponging. Circa 1890. *Value:* $110.00-$130.00+.

A very unusual circular trivet or hot plate, 7" diameter, ½" thick. Circa 1890. *Value:* $60.00-$80.00+.

Various views of a stunning Roseville Pottery pitcher and basin set in the Colonial pattern. The pitcher measures 11" high, while the bowl is 4" high and 16½" in diameter. Note the relief-molded organic designs as well as the gold highlighting on both pieces. Circa early 1900s. *Value:* $250.00-$300.00+ for the set.

5½" high pitcher with strong brown and green sponging over cream-colored earthenware. Circa 1915.

Miniature pitcher and basin decorated with multicolored or "rainbow" spatter. Pitcher is 3¾" high, basin is 6" in diameter. *Value:* $275.00-$350.00.

Some Additional Spatterware Prices

Bowl, Tulip pattern, 18" in diameter, blue spatter, $275.00-$325.00

Chamber pot, Rose pattern, blue spatter decoration, $225.00-$275.00

Creamer, rainbow spatter, 5¼" high, $150.00-$200.00

Cup and saucer, Schoolhouse pattern, $525.00-$600.00

Cup and saucer, Thistle pattern, $200.00-$250.00

Miniature mug, Peafowl pattern with blue spattering, 2½" high, $450.00-$500.00.

Pitcher, rainbow spatter, 12" high, $275.00-$325.00.

Plate, Acorn pattern, 9½" diameter, $350.00-$400.00.

Plate, Castle pattern, 8½" diameter, red spatter, $375.00-$425.00.

Plate, Star pattern, 8½" diameter, $200.00-$250.00.

Salt cellar, 2½" high, blue spatter, $100.00-$125.00.

Soap dish, green spatter, $90.00-$110.00.

Teapot, yellow and red rainbow spatter, 6" high, $700.00-$750.00.

Wash bowl and pitcher, Peafowl pattern, multicolored spatter work, $800.00-$1000.00

Bibliography

The Antique Trader Antiques & Collectibles Price Guide.
Dubuque, Iowa, The Babka Publishing Co., 1986.

Huxford, Sharon and Bob. *The Collectors Encyclopedia of Roseville Pottery.* Paducah, Kentucky: Collector Books, 1984.

Ketchum, William C., Jr. *Pottery and Porcelain.* New York, Alfred A. Knopf, 1983.

McClinton, Katharine Morrison. *A Handbook of Popular Antiques.* New York: Bonanza Books, 1946.

Savage, George and Newman, Harold. *An Illustrated Dictionary of Ceramics.* London, Thames and Hudson, 1985.

Warman's Antiques and their Prices. Elkins Park, PA: Warman Publishing Co., Inc., 1984.

Shouldered mixing bowl with pink and blue sponging on yellowware. 5″ high, 9½″ rim diameter. Circa 1920. *Value:* $40.00-$60.00.